JUST
Imagine

Other books in the
NEVILLE GODDARD SERIES
by J Watier:

I Am: The Wisdom of Neville Goddard in
Today's Language

Neville Goddard Quotes by Subject

God Is Looking In The Mirror

JUST
Imagine

J Watier

The Wisdom of
Neville Goddard

In Today's Language

Cover design and layout by J Watier

Original artwork: "Round Rainbow" by Black Moon (Shutter-
stock 176773136)

Contents

Foreword

When I first came across Neville Goddard's teachings, I was hooked. I read everything I could find, resonating powerfully with the truth they contained. His teaching underscored the wisdom I've gleaned from so many other spiritual teachers. I began jotting down quotes and filling notebooks with my thoughts. Though I was moved by the content of his work, the wording was outdated, so I found myself paraphrasing sections to better grasp the meaning.

This book brings those paraphrased lines together in a way that sums up Neville's teaching about imagination. The direct quotes (set apart in italics) that I have included are accurate in word, however, I took some liberties in the use of punctuation—where I felt it made the quote more compelling, and in the use of gender-neutral pronouns—to make the truths of his teaching more inclusive. The stories (case studies) contained in this book are also paraphrased from Neville's books and lectures. I have assigned names to some of the characters, summarized the original piece, and/or compiled details from various sources—all for ease of reading.

My desire is that Neville's teachings, expressed in more up-to-date English, will help you as much as they have helped me. As you allow his words to seep into your very being, I hope you start to feel the power of your wonderful imagination.

—J Watier

Introduction

"Imagination is the very gateway of reality."

—Awakened Imagination

There are words that have been so misused, so over-extended, they don't mean much of anything at all. Imagination is one of those words. It encompasses all sorts of ideas, some of them directly opposed to one another. It can stand for fancy, thought, hallucination, suspicion, and more. Its use is so wide and its meaning so varied, that the word *imagination* has lost its status and significance. But what if imagination is something else altogether?

Absolutely nothing appears or continues to be by its own power. The power has to come from somewhere, from something. Many attribute these happenings to God or the Universe or some other name given to a power or being they believe to be outside themselves.

In the following pages, you'll see that events happen because comparatively stable imaginal activities created them, and they continue to be only as long as they receive that support. But what, exactly, is this imaginative power, and how does it work?

The story of a young Neville's trip to his family home in Barbados can be seen as a template for examining the various facets of imagination. The powerful elements contained within this story are keys to understanding and applying the same life-changing wisdom that he received from his friend and mentor, Abdullah. It was wisdom that Neville implemented in his own life and then went on to share with the world.

Neville's words and stories, paraphrased in this book, will solve the mystery of imagining. They'll show you the secret of causation—that imagining creates reality.

Imagination is your ability to perceive something that right now seems to be other than you, something that feels apart from you. The drama of life is imaginal, not physical. The world you live in is a world of imagination, and it's through your imaginal activities that you initiate the circumstances that play out in your world.

And when you learn to control what you're imagining, you can know what is in the process of becoming. You can see the future!

Neville uses the Bible as a guidebook for living, translating the often confusing scripture verses—that were only ever intended as symbolism—into clear and simple truths. He shows you that God (which is your consciousness, your awareness of being) is the one and only creator. And that your wonderful human imagination is God in action.

> *"Wherever (your) attitude to life is truly imaginative, there (you) and God are merged in creative unity."*
>
> —Truth (Radio Talk)

Just Imagine

Winter in Barbados

"To one's imagination, all things are possible."

—Five Lessons

In November 1933, Neville said goodbye to his parents in New York City as they sailed home to Barbados. He'd been in the United States for twelve years and hadn't found the success he was looking for. He'd been in theatre where he made money one year and spent it the next month. He wasn't by their standards, or his, a successful person. He was ashamed to go home because other members of his family had done very well for themselves. After a dozen years in America he was a failure in his own eyes.

When he said goodbye to his parents, he had no desire to go to Barbados, yet as the ship pulled out and he walked back up the street, that very desire possessed him.

He was unemployed and had no place to go except a little room on 75th Street, so he went straight to his old friend Abdullah and told him about the sudden urge. The teacher asked Neville one simple question.

"What do you want?"

Neville reiterated that he'd like to spend the winter in Barbados and then added that he was broke.

Abdullah's reply was, "If you want to go, Neville, you have gone." Neville didn't understand and asked him to explain.

Abdullah probed further. "Do you really want to go?" Neville's answer was a definitive yes.

"If you will imagine yourself to be in Barbados," Abdullah said, "thinking and viewing the world from that state of consciousness instead of thinking *of* Barbados, you will spend the winter there."

Neville listened, but there was still doubt on his face.

"Do not ask me how you are going to go," Abdullah responded. "You are in Barbados. You do not ask how when you are already there. You ARE there. Now you walk as though you were there."

He told Neville that if he could occupy the state of consciousness of already being in Barbados, the state of consciousness would devise the means best suited to realize itself. Abdullah instructed him to walk out the door and instead of walking on 72nd Street in New York City, he was to walk on the palm-lined streets of Barbados.

Abdullah wasn't the kind of person you argued with, so Neville did as the teacher said. He went out of his place in a daze, saying, "I am in Barbados. I have no money, I have no job, I am not even well clothed, and yet I am in Barbados."

Two weeks later, Neville was no nearer to his goal than the day he first told Abdullah about his desire, so he said to his friend, "Ab, I trust you implicitly, but I can't see how it is going to work. I still don't have any money."

Abdullah rose from his chair, went to his study, and slammed the door, saying, "I have said all that I have to say."

The message was clear. Neville knew he had to radically adjust his thoughts. He had to go beyond the limits of his senses, beyond what his present state was telling him. He had to find the feeling of already being in Barbados and view the world from that standpoint.

Abdullah had emphasized the importance of the state a person views the world from as they fall asleep, citing the prophets of old who claimed to hear the voice of God in their dreams. So that night and several nights following, Neville fell asleep imagining that he was in his father's house in Barbados.

On December 3rd, Neville went to Abdullah again, admitting that he wasn't any closer to realizing his desire. The very last ship that would get him to Barbados for Christmas sailed at noon on December 6th.

The teacher simply repeated his statement, "You ARE in Barbados, Neville."

On the morning of December 4th, having no job and no place to go, Neville slept late. When he got up, there was a letter under his door. It was from Barbados. As he opened it, a little piece of paper flickered to the floor. It was a check for fifty dollars. The letter was from his brother who was insistent that the family should all be together for Christmas, as they had never all been in the same house since they'd become adults.

Neville's brother knew he wasn't working and explained in the letter that the money was for some new clothes and shoes. Then he added that he would cover the full cost of the trip, including incidentals. He'd contacted the shipping line in New York and told them to issue Neville a ticket when he arrived at their office.

Neville went as instructed, but they told him they didn't have any space left on the December 6th sailing to Barbados. The best they could do was issue a third-class fare taking him from New York to St. Thomas. At that point, Neville could move to first class, as a few passengers were disembarking. They added that even though he was traveling third class for part of the journey, he could enjoy the first-class dining room and decks for the entire voyage.

Neville agreed to take it. He went back to Abdullah that afternoon and told him what he'd done, thinking his friend would be happy. But his friend's response surprised him.

"Who told you that you are going third class? Did I see you in Barbados, the man you are, going third class? You ARE in Barbados, and you went there first class!"

Neville didn't see Abdullah again before he sailed for Barbados two days later. When he reached the dock with his passport and papers to get aboard the ship, the agent said to him, "We have good news for you, Mr. Goddard. There's been a cancellation. We've moved you to first class."

New York City is as far from Barbados in similarity as it is in distance, yet Neville did as he was told and walked the streets of New York as though he walked the streets of Barbados. He slept in his bed as if he slept in his father's house. He walked and slept and ate, imagining he was actually there. He could almost smell the fragrance of those coconut-lined lanes as he created in his mind's eye the atmosphere he would physically encounter if he were in Barbados with his family.

And as he remained as faithful as he could to that assumption—even though he saw no evidence—things began to work on his behalf.

His brother in Barbados had never before mentioned the idea of Neville coming home. He wasn't the type to make such demands of his younger sibling. Yet suddenly he had the urge to have the family together, and he had the means to make it happen—all the while believing the whole idea originated with him. Somebody else canceled their passage at the last minute and Neville, through no effort of his own, received the benefit of it.

So Neville went home to Barbados, enjoyed three wonderful months with his family, and then returned first class. He even brought back a nice sum of cash. A trip like that, had he paid for it, would have cost him a small fortune, yet he did it without a nickel in his pocket.

The Voice of Desire

*"The spiritual (self) speaks to the natural
(self) through the language of desire. The
key to progress in life and to the fulfillment
of dreams lies in the ready obedience
to its voice."*

—Five Lessons

One of the first things you learn in the Barbados story is that the desire came to Neville suddenly. He told his friend, Abdullah, that the experience had been strange, that the urge had somehow possessed him.

That's because desire is the driving force of all action. You couldn't move a finger unless you had a desire to move it. No matter what you do, you are following the desire that, in the moment, dominates your mind.

Desire springs from a place deep within you. It comes from a part of you that has already seen and tasted your sought-after ideals. And it brings with it the awareness of ultimate attainment. You couldn't have a desire unless it contained its own plan of self-expression.

When you have a desire, it's the infinite YOU (God in you) that is speaking. Through the language of desire you're being urged to accept what *isn't* as though it *is*. Desire is your deepest communion with yourself. It's YOU telling yourself that what you want is yours, now! You prove your acceptance of this fact by adjusting your mind to the truth of it. Your desires are the living, active words of God, and they come to you with the promise of fulfillment.

> *"Desire exists to be gratified in the activity of imagination."*
> —Awakened Imagination

Desire is a good thing. It's a right and natural craving that finds satisfaction in higher and higher states of consciousness. Life is the appeasement of hunger, and there are infinite states of consciousness you can view the world from that will satisfy that hunger. Each state contains the element of desire, uniquely designed to lift you to greater levels of experience.

There's nothing wrong with your desire to transcend your present state. There'd be no progress if it weren't for your dissatisfaction with your current condition. It's natural for you to seek a more rich and beautiful life; it's right that you wish for greater understanding, greater health, greater security. The creative desire is innate within you.

Desires always have some personal gain in view. The greater the anticipated gain, the more intense the desire. There is no absolutely unselfish desire. When there is nothing to gain, there is no desire, and consequently no action.

So stop asking yourself whether you are worthy to receive what you desire. You didn't create the desire. It was born within you because of what you're conscious of being. If you're aware of being hungry, you automatically desire food. If you're imprisoned, literally or figuratively, you naturally desire freedom. Desires are automatic, and they live within you until they are realized.

> *"The purpose of life is the creative realization of desire."*
> —The Law and the Promise

Just Imagine

What Do You Want?

*"(We) can be anything in this world we
desire to be if we will clearly define our aim
in life and constantly occupy that aim."*
—Changing the Feeling of "I" (Lecture)

When Neville went to see his friend to tell him of his sudden desire, the wise teacher asked two simple questions. The first was, "What do you want?" In response, Neville expanded the scope of his desire, saying that he wanted to spend the entire winter in Barbados.

A question like that seems redundant when the desire has already been stated or is obvious. The same question is asked numerous times in the New Testament. Its purpose is to emphasize the importance of defining your goal.

Without a goal in life, you'll drift. Paul describes this in Philippians: "But one thing I do, forgetting those things which are behind and reaching forward

11

to those things which are ahead, I press toward the goal…" (Philippians 3:13-14) It's the lack of passionate direction in life that causes you to fail. In fact, that's what the Bible calls sin.

> *"Sin means missing one's mark in life,*
> *falling short of one's ideal, failing to*
> *achieve one's aim."*
> —Awakened Imagination

In defining your aim, you have to truly want it—and that was Abdullah's next question: "Do you really want to go?"

The author of Psalms describes his passion in this poetic way: "As the deer pants for the water brooks, so pants my soul for You, O God." (Psalms 42:1) With all your heart you have to want to be different than you are or have something different than you have. This passion is a concentrated, burning desire—something you hunger and thirst after.

As powerful as it is, however, desire itself has no reality. It's just a conduit, a springboard, a driving force. Your awareness of being (which is God) is the only reality. Things only live as long as you're aware of being or possessing them, so to realize your desire, your ideal must be fixed in your consciousness. That's where it finds expression. And in order to give it expression, you have to fully identify with it.

"Willingly identify yourself with that which you most desire, knowing that it will find expression through you. Yield to the feeling of the wish fulfilled and be consumed as its victim."

—The Power of Awareness

Just Imagine

Creation Is Done

*"Creation is finished, and what we
call creativeness is really only a deeper
receptiveness or keener susceptibility on
our part."*

—Meditation (Radio Talk)

The words that initially confused Neville, "If you want to go, you have gone," hold one of the most powerful revelations: Creation is done. Abdullah never talked about what *might* happen. In his mind, the voyage had already taken place. His friend was IN Barbados.

The world of creation is finished, and its blueprint is within you. You saw it before you came to this earth plane, and you've been trying to remember it and activate sections of it ever since.

There are infinite aspects of it. Your task is to choose the right one, and then by determined focus, play it out in your imagination. By assembling the right sequence and experiencing that sequence in your imagination

15

until it has the tones of reality, you consciously create circumstances. It's impossible to force anything into being; you can only ever imagine things into being.

> *"The entire contents of all time and all space, while experienced in a time sequence, actually coexist in an infinite and eternal now."*
> —The Power of Awareness

The inner world of thought and feeling that your imagination can tune to has real structure. It exists in its own higher space. That is why you can identify with it.

Movement within that space is purely causal; your body and your physical world respond to what's going on within. They are simply a reflection of that higher realm.

But even though creation is finished and exists on a higher plane, you still get to partake in the creative process. And you do that through imagination imbued with feeling.

The mechanism of creation is hidden in the depths of your subconscious, which is the womb of creation, and it transcends reason. It regards a feeling as a fact, and on this assumption proceeds to give expression to it.

As you wake up to your true power and your true identity, you join in this process in a deliberate way through your imagination.

The creative process begins as a desire, continues as a feeling, and crescendos in a cinematic production, an imaginal act that has all the clarity and feeling of reality. That's where your involvement ends. The rest unfolds as naturally as the sun rises or your heart beats.

All you can possibly need or desire is already yours. Every possible situation can be seen as a ready-made state. Every detail, every plot, is already worked out, but it's excluded from view because you can see only the contents of your own consciousness.

It's your assumptions—what you determine to be true even though there's no rational basis for it—that restore your vision. The world doesn't change; it's only your assumptions that change. You create nothing, but your assumptions determine what parts of creation you'll experience.

Before he went to see his friend, Neville was focused on very limited aspects of creation—the cold New York streets and his dire financial situation. Barbados was completely excluded from his view. Abdullah helped him to expand his vision and thereby fulfill his desire.

> *"The whole of creation exists in you, and it is your destiny to become increasingly aware of its infinite wonders and to experience ever greater and grander portions of it."*
>
> —The Power of Awareness

Don't Ask How

*"Imagination and faith are the only
faculties of the mind needed to create
objective conditions."*

—Prayer, The Art of Believing

You don't ask how to get somewhere if you're already there!

Abdullah's statement to Neville was as logical as a statement can be, yet so many get tripped up there. It's not your job to determine the path. Your desire comes with it's own distinctive plan of self-expression—and trying to figure it out or applying effort to get it to happen faster just messes with the process and prolongs the results.

Your job, as was Neville's, is to have faith, to stay true to your vision. Imagination will serve you. It is powerful, but it isn't obligated to produce only good and perfect results. It exercises its absolute freedom by giving you choices, by allowing you free will to follow good or evil (*evil* in the Bible is the same as sin—it's failure to stay true to your desires).

Once you've made your choice, and your ideal begins to feel natural to you, then imagination wields its infinite power and wisdom by shaping your sensuous outer world, conforming it to the pattern of your well-rehearsed inner drama.

To get to that place of feeling natural in your vision, you need to have faith in your unseen claim. A little faith, if persisted in, will grow to become a conviction. A conviction is a powerful assumption. And assumptions are what your imagination feeds on.

"We must act on the assumption that we already possess that which we desire, for all that we desire is already present within us. It only waits to be claimed."

—Answered Prayer

Faith is believing what is unbelievable. Faith is confidence, and confidence will reward you greatly. When you assume that you already have what you desire, you're committing yourself to the feeling of the wish fulfilled in faith that it will become a reality. And it must become a reality because imagining creates reality.

Without faith it's impossible to realize anything. It's through faith that your world is framed. "Now faith is the substance of things hoped for, the evidence of things not seen." (Hebrews 11:1)

"Imagination is the beginning of the growth of all forms, and faith is the substance out of which they are formed. By imagination, that which exists in latency or is asleep within the deep of consciousness is awakened and is given form."

—Prayer, The Art of Believing

Just Imagine

Occupy The State

*"Imagination must center itself in some
state and view the world from that state."*

—Awakened Imagination

A state is all that you believe and consent to as true. Your 3D world is a revelation of the states that your imagination is currently fused with. No idea can be realized unless your mind accepts it. Full acceptance of the state you're identified with results in the fusion of your imagination with it. And this fusion is what shapes the world as you know it. Yet so many fail to occupy the states they desire.

Perpetual construction, deferred occupancy—it's a common condition. But why build a house and not live there? Why dream and not occupy your dreams?

The secret of those who lie in bed awake, dreaming things true, is that they know how to occupy their dream, to live in it until, in fact, they do just that.

Living in your dream means thinking *from* it, not just thinking *of* it.

> *"Every state is already there as mere*
> *possibility as long as you think of it but*
> *is overpoweringly real when you think*
> *from it."*
>
> —Awakened Imagination

Once you accept a state and fuse to it with your imagination, you are thinking from it. Abdullah told Neville it wasn't enough to think *about* Barbados. He needed to occupy the state of consciousness of already *being* there. He instructed him to walk down the streets of New York City, imagining he was walking down the palm-lined streets of his tropical island home, because he knew that the state you think from determines the world you live in.

You have to experience in imagination what you would experience in the flesh if you already achieved your desire, if you were physically where you want to be. In other words, you make elsewhere *here* and the future *now*.

When you do, your Infinite Self will use whatever means necessary to bring about that state in a way your physical senses can appreciate and others around you can witness.

"If you are dissatisfied with your present expression in life, the only way to change it is to take your attention away from that which seems so real to you and rise in consciousness to that which you desire to be."

—At Your Command

The opposite is also true. If you detach from a state (and you can at any moment), the conditions and circumstances that made that union real start to vanish. The fusion of your imagination with any state is a temporary joining of two entities. When you shift your consciousness (i.e. withdraw your imagination from one state and join it to another) the conditions associated with the first union must vanish.

You live by committing yourself to invisible states, by fusing your imagination with something that seems to be apart from you, and in doing so you experience the results of that fusion. But it's important to choose wisely. All states are lifeless until your imagination fuses with them.

The only way you can lose (or change) what you have is by detaching from the state where the things you are experiencing have their life. For Neville, his current condition—spending the winter in New York with no money—vanished in the vivid light of his persistent dreams. He was able to detach his imagination from his present state and match it to a higher concept, thereby rising above his current limitations.

> *"Our imagination connects us with the state desired. But we must use imagination masterfully, not as an onlooker thinking of the end, but as a partaker thinking from the end."*
>
> —Awakened Imagination

You have to be there in imagination. You have to live in the end. It's a mental journey into a desired state. Your inner world has to become more real to you than the world around you. Your dreams and visions need to be as vibrant as the elements of nature. It's this imaginary experience (partaking of the end with full acceptance of its reality) that is the vehicle to manifestation.

Desire is thinking *of*. Satisfaction is thinking *from*. And imagination is the bridge between the two. You need to move yourself mentally from one to the other. You can't get there by reason. Reason, by its very nature, is restricted to the evidence of the senses. But imagination has no such limitation. It will take you there.

Thinking from the end is determined imagination. You have to abandon yourself completely to your wish fulfilled for your love of that state. In doing so, you live in the new state and no longer in the old one.

The world is a manifestation of the mental activity that goes on within you, so it's important to control the "ends" that you think from. You need to design end scenes that match the pattern of your fulfilled desire. The future must become the present in your imagination if you want to wisely and consciously create your circumstances. You have to translate vision into being, thinking of into thinking from. Thinking from the end is intense perception. It's creative living.

If in your imagination you can spend time in the end you desire, you can be confident that you'll be there in the flesh one day. It's not just reasonable probability. Deliberate, continuous use of your imagination, saturated with positive feeling, will cause your assumptions to harden into facts.

> *"To realize your desire, an action must start in your imagination, apart from the evidence of the senses, involving movement of self and implying fulfillment of your desire."*
>
> —Awakened Imagination

If you want to see your desire manifest, it helps to create a passive state, a meditative state similar to the feeling just before you fall asleep. In this relaxed condition—where you feel drowsy but are still able to control your thoughts—your mind can more easily accept the reality of a subjective state.

Start by relaxing in a comfortable chair or on a bed. Close your eyes and imagine that you're sleepy. A far-away feeling begins to envelop you. You're pleasantly, comfortably at rest, with no need to move or shift your body. Now start to imagine.

Focus on your objective. Bring it so close that you can feel it—but not just in a warm, fuzzy, "wouldn't it be nice" sense. Entertain specific images that match your desire. What does it look like? How many small details can you make out? What would it feel like if you were to touch or hold your desire? How does it smell? Is there a sound associated with it? Is there a movement or action you can participate in?

Spiritual sensation is imaginal sight, sound, scent, taste, and touch that you infuse into your mental drama to give the scene sensory vividness. Step into the fullness of the sensory details and bask in the sensation of being or having what you desire now.

When you do this, you experience your future *now* in your imagination. The future event *is* a reality now in a dimensionally larger world. With your imagination you've made the two equivalent. You've matched your imagination to a state that already preexists. You have traveled via imagination to that larger world to experience it.

It's an exercise in bilocation—being in two places simultaneously. You are in one place in your imagination and another place physically. This practice develops your power of concentration and allows you to achieve waking consciousness in the inner, expansive world.

"Enter the image of the wish fulfilled, then give it sensory vividness and tones of reality by mentally acting as you would act were it a physical fact."
—The Law and the Promise

Once you feel yourself into this relaxed state, once you've experienced your imaginary environment with all your inner senses, now you step into the predetermined action—an action or event that implies you already are or have what you want. Mentally construct a scene you believe would naturally follow the fulfillment of your desire.

Feel it in the moment. You can't just see it happening at a distance. You have to feel that you're performing the action here and now so that the imaginary sensation is real to you. The key is to be physically still and mentally active.

Enter into the imaginary action like you're an actor playing the part. Let other "actors" reflect to you what you're projecting. Imagine them seeing you and responding to you just like they would if you already were (or possessed) what you desire.

Keep it simple. Condense the idea into a single act, and then re-enact it over and over again. If your attention wanders, bring it back to its task, and keep on doing that until the imaginary action takes on the textures of reality.

> *"Inner action orders all things according to the nature of itself."*
> —Awakened Imagination

If you want a promotion at work, imagine the congratulatory handshake from your boss and notice the firm grip of his hand. Feel the slight jolt of a friendly hand on your shoulder. See your friends' and coworkers' smiles and feel their sincerity. Engage in conversation as if you were right there celebrating your promotion!

If you want to be married, imagine the feel of the ring on your finger. Touch it. Turn it around. Pull it over your knuckle, then slip it back in place.

If you're a teacher or speaker wanting an audience, feel your hands grip the podium, hear the crowd's applause fill the auditorium, or hear your agent call informing you of a sold-out tour.

If it's improved health you seek, ask yourself what kinds of things you'd be doing if you were vibrantly healthy. Then take that action in your imagination.

It's not enough to desire success or abundance. What would you be doing if you *were* those things now? Do that in imagination.

If it's a physical presence you want to manifest, a friend or significant other, imagine they're standing in front of you. Reach out and touch them. Take them in your imaginary arms. Virtual touch is powerful. If you can feel your hand on them, they're real. Keep enjoying that experience, and they have no choice but to physically show up in your world.

> *"When the feeling of reality is yours, for the moment at least, you are mentally impotent. The desire to repeat the act...is lost, having been replaced by the feeling of accomplishment."*
> —Five Lessons

You might be wondering how much time you should spend in the imaginal act or how often you should do it. The first answer is: You engage in the imaginal act, abandoning yourself to it, until satisfaction is reached. When you feel sated and complete, when you're basking in the NOWness of your desire, you're done.

You can't continue wanting what you already have. If you assume you are what you desire to be to the point of satisfaction, you no longer want it. If you don't reach that place of fulfillment, repeat the mental action over again until you feel as though you've touched the fullness of it.

When you open your eyes and emerge from a successful meditation, you should feel like you just watched the happy and pleasing end of a movie (even though you didn't see how the end came about).

Knowing the end of a movie, you can now go back and watch the whole movie, and regardless of any drama or uncomfortable scenes, you'll remain calm and secure in the knowledge that the end has already been defined.

If you are asking the second question—how often to do the process—you're not getting this. You need to BE not DO.

There are many factors that contribute to the length of time it takes to manifest a desire—particularly your self-concept and your understanding and belief in the process. But if you truly find fulfillment and satisfaction in the mental act, it won't seem like work.

So the simple answer is: BE your ideal. Assume that identity. Stay there because it feels good, and you'll be actively participating in the fulfillment of your desire.

> *"Where the consciousness is placed, you
> do not have to take the physical body; it
> gravitates there in spite of you. Things*

happen to compel you to move in the direction where you are consciously dwelling."

—Five Lessons

The Bible says, "I go to prepare a place for you. And if I go and prepare a place for you, I will come again and receive you to Myself, that where I am, there you may be also." (John 14:2-3)

This verse is talking about imagination. You are your imagination. Therefore, you have to be where you are in imagination.

If you sit quietly and assume you're somewhere else, you've gone ahead and prepared that place. When you open your eyes, the bilocation you created vanishes, and you're back in the physical form you left behind. Nevertheless, you prepared the place, and in time you'll dwell there in the flesh.

Neville slept in his father's house in Barbados. He walked the palm-lined streets. And because he did that preparation in his imagination, he set himself on the path that would take him there physically.

Just Imagine

Ignore What Is

*"In the world of sense, we see what we have
to see; in the world of imagination, we see
what we want to see; And seeing it, we
create it for the world of sense to see."*

—The Law and the Promise

There are two outlooks on life that everyone pos-
sesses—a natural focus and a spiritual focus. The
first is ordinary waking consciousness, governed by
your senses, and the second is a controlled imagination, governed by desire.

You might argue that you have no choice but to be
ruled by your physical senses because they are real.
But nothing is real beyond the imaginative pattern
you make of it. A sensory impression is just a mental
image. In that way, it's no different than a thought or
a memory. What makes your senses so objectively real
is that you've trained your imagination to function *in*
them and think *from* them.

Imagination can be both conservative and transformative. It's conservative when it builds its world

from images supplied by memory and the evidence of the senses. It's transformative when it conjures things as they ought to be, building its world from the infinite realm of possibility.

> *"One must adopt either the way of imagination or the way of sense. No compromise or neutrality is possible."*
> —The Law and the Promise

In the New Testament, Jesus says, "He who is not with Me is against Me." (Matthew 12:30) The *me* in this verse is your imagination. And to be *against* your imagination is to be seduced by your senses. If you passively surrender to the evidence of your senses, you underestimate the capacity of your Inner Self.

If you want to escape your sense fixation and transform your life into the dream of what could be, you need a controlled imagination. It's through imagination that you escape the limitations of your senses and the restrictions your reasoning mind places on you.

Neville had to go beyond the limits of his senses—the cold he felt in his fingers as he walked the streets of New York, the treeless urban landscape of Manhattan. He had to go beyond what his present state was telling him—that he didn't have a job nor the money he'd need for a trip to Barbados. He had to see past the harsh reality of his world, and the only way he could do that was through imagination.

First Class All The Way

"...dreams are realized not by the rich, but by the imaginative."

—The Law and the Promise

After acknowledging his desire to spend the winter in Barbados, and imagining it to the point of fulfillment, Neville gladly accepted a third-class ticket home to see his family—as most people would have done under the circumstances. He went back to tell his friend what had happened, supposing that he'd be thrilled by the turn of events. But Abdullah's response was not what Neville expected. The evidence Neville presented him with didn't match what Abdullah had been imagining for his friend.

There are an infinite number of possible states you can imagine and thereby experience. To experience a state, your beliefs have to be a match to it. Neville, for many years, had been used to seeing himself in reduced circumstances, so a third-class ticket was a match to that set of beliefs. But he'd also experienced abundance and ultimately would have preferred to travel first class. Abdullah knew the importance of remaining faithful to an idea and not compromising. Neville may have wavered somewhat, but Abdullah stayed true to the assumption that his friend was in Barbados and that he'd traveled there in luxury.

This reveals two important truths. The first is that you don't have to settle. You don't have to accept the idea of lack. The Bible is filled with stories confirming this.

One of the most famous is the story of water turned to wine. Jesus said to his mother (when she pointed out the situation of lack at a family wedding), "Woman, what have I to do with thee?" (John 2:4)

At first glance, this sounds like Jesus, the embodiment of love, is being rude to his mother—until you understand that you are Jesus, and your mother is your own consciousness.

You are creatures of habit, accepting the evidence of your senses as final verdicts. (If wine is needed for the guests and your senses tell you there's no wine, you accept this lack as final.) But when you remember that your consciousness is the one and only reality, when you deny the evidence of your senses and assume the consciousness of having what you need, you have in essence rebuked your mother (or the consciousness that suggested lack).

*"As well as (for) yourself, claim for others
their divine inheritance."*
—The Power of Awareness

The second truth revealed is that your influence over another person is significant. You can see good *in* others and *for* others. You can influence them to confidence, health, well-being, and more by your sincere assumptions about them.

Abdullah saw the man that Neville was: a good man, a dignified man. He also had his own high standards of living and of travel. Therefore he could imagine no less than first class for his young friend.

He held that assumption without wavering, and Neville, because he was open to the good that could come to him, and because they matched the desires he ultimately held for himself, became the beneficiary of his friend's determined thoughts.

*"All imaginative men and women are
forever casting forth enchantments, and
all passive men and women, who have no
powerful imaginative lives, are continually
passing under the spell of their power."*
—The Law and the Promise

Just Imagine

A Bridge of Incidents

"An assumption builds a bridge of incidents that leads inevitably to the fulfillment of itself."

—The Power of Awareness

Once you've experienced in imagination what you'd experience in the flesh if you achieved your goal, and you've done it with all the richness and precision of reality—then you can confidently, joyfully follow the course of time until you inevitably meet your goal and live it precisely the way you experienced it in your imagination.

Things all around you will conspire to assist you on your journey. Looking back, you'll be able to see the subtle threads that led you to your goal.

You'll see, too, that you could never have devised the means that your imagination employed to fulfill itself. Those subtle threads form a bridge, a series of events that unfold in what some might call miraculous ways.

A miracle, however, is just a name given to the works of imagination by people who have no knowledge of its power and function. It's a name given to the works of faith by those who have no faith.

By sleeping in his family home in his imagination as if he were sleeping there in the flesh, Neville fused his imagination with the state, and therefore he had to experience that state in the flesh also. Thinking from the end, from the feeling and assumption of his wish fulfilled, was the source of everything that happened—everything that appeared as outer cause. Imagination was the cause, and everything else was the result.

The Bible says, "For My thoughts are not your thoughts, nor are your ways My ways." (Isaiah 55:8) "How unsearchable are His judgments and His ways past finding out." (Romans 11:33) This is your imagination speaking (and being spoken of). Imagination has ways and means you could never know, and it devises the route to its intended end without your help.

> "Others give reality to what were...mere
> figments of (the) imagination."
> —The Law and the Promise

Your dimensionally greater Self takes your assumption as a command and influences circumstances and events, including the behavior of others.

In Neville's case, it spanned the Atlantic and prompted his brother to write that letter. It caused someone else to cancel their first-class passage. It did all the things necessary to take Neville physically where his imagination had already gone. Everything acted in harmony with his assumption.

He didn't need to go to the shipping company to plead his case. He didn't have to ask them to bump someone who was in first class so that he could travel as his brother (and Abdullah) had intended. He didn't need to write his brother asking for extra money for clothes. Through imagination, and imagination alone, he predetermined his future.

> *"Our acceptance of the waking dream
> as physical reality wills the means for its
> fulfillment."*
> —Out of This World

A bridge of incidents is what follows any imaginative experience, good or bad. But for that chain of events to unfold favorably, you have to be aware of *being* what you were formerly aware of *wanting.* You have to accept it as reality.

Then you'll enjoy the delicious feeling of fulfillment. You'll embrace the satisfaction. Your desire will have been quenched, even though the manifestation has yet to happen. You walk across the bridge in the certainty that it's done because you've seen and felt the end that you desire. You're confident that it will be, so you go on with your life in joyful expectancy.

Case Studies

The following stories, demonstrating the effective use of imagination, are paraphrased from Neville's books and lectures. Names have been assigned to some of the characters, and details have been summarized and/or compiled from various sources for better flow and ease of reading.

Just Imagine

AN HONORABLE DISCHARGE

"When, through concentrated attention,
our desire appears to possess the
distinctness and feeling of reality; when
the form of thought is as vivid as the form
of nature, we have given it the right to
become a visible fact in our lives."

—The Law of Assumption

In the spring of 1943, Neville was 38 years old and stationed at a large army camp in Louisiana. He very badly wanted to get out of the army, but only if it was in an honorable way.

The only way to do that was to apply for a discharge, and the application had to be approved by his commanding officer. According to army regulations, the decision of the commanding officer was final and couldn't be appealed. Neville, following the necessary procedure, applied for a discharge. Within four hours, his application was returned, disapproved.

Since he was unable to appeal the decision, he turned to the "higher power" of his own conscious-ness. He knew what he wanted, and he didn't need to ask anyone's permission. He knew that his conscious-ness was the only reality, that whatever state of con-sciousness he was focused on determined the events he'd encounter.

That night, in the moments between getting into his army cot and falling asleep, Neville concentrated on the reality he wanted to experience. He imagined himself in his apartment in New York City. He clearly visualized the apartment, vividly picturing each room with all its furnishings.

Lying flat on his back, he completely relaxed his body, inducing a state that was bordering on sleep, while at the same time being in control of his focus. In his mind, he was in his own room in his own apart-ment, lying on his own bed. His wife and his little daughter were there, asleep.

In his imagination, he got up and walked from room to room, touching various pieces of furniture. Then he went to the window and, with his hands rest-ing on the sill, looked out at the street. His imagina-tion was so vivid that he could see the details in the pavement, the trees, and the familiar red brick of the building across the street.

He then returned to his imaginal bed and felt him-self drifting off to sleep. Every part of his imaginal experience was based on the premise that he was no longer in the army. At the point of falling asleep, his consciousness was filled with the assumption that he was home—and not just on furlough—he was honorably discharged and living there as a civilian.

For the next eight nights, Neville slept in his bed in New York City. On the ninth day, orders came from headquarters requesting him to fill out a new application for discharge. Shortly after he did it, he was ordered to report to the colonel's office. The colonel asked him if he still wanted to get out of the army. Neville said yes. The commanding officer told Neville that while he disagreed with his decision, he had decided to set aside his objections and approve the discharge. Within hours, Neville was on a train headed for New York.

Just Imagine

BACK TO BARBADOS

"We should...deliberately disentangle our
minds from the evidence of the senses and
focus our attention on an invisible state,
mentally feeling it and sensing it until it
has all the distinctness of reality."

—Five Lessons

In January 1946, Neville took his wife and little daughter back to Barbados for a holiday. He wasn't aware when he booked the trip that there would be difficulties getting a return passage, so he didn't think to reserve it before leaving New York.

When they arrived in Barbados he discovered that there were only two ships serving the islands, one from Boston and one from New York, and there was no available space on either ship before September. He had commitments in New York the first week in May, so he put his name on the long waiting list for the April sailing.

A few days later, the ship from New York was still anchored in the harbor. Observing it carefully, Neville decided it was the ship they would take on their trip home in April. His desire was clear. Back in their hotel room, he began mentally creating the inner action that would match his fulfilled desire. Settling in an easy chair in the bedroom, he began to lose himself in this imaginative activity.

In Barbados, it's necessary to take a smaller boat to get out to the large ship. Neville knew he needed to capture the feeling of being on that ship, so he chose the inner action of stepping from the small boat onto the gangplank of the steamer.

The first time he tried, his attention wandered as he ascended the gangplank. He brought himself down and tried again. And again. He lost track of how many times he carried out the action in his imagination, but he continued determinedly until he was able to reach the deck.

Then he looked back at the port, feeling the sweet sadness of leaving his island home. He was happy to be returning to New York, but nostalgic about saying goodbye to family and friends. He continued walking the gangplank and feeling the nostalgia until he dozed off. When he woke up, he went about the usual activities of the day.

The next morning, he received a call from the steamship company requesting him to come down to their office and pick up tickets for the April sailing, as there had been a cancellation.

He was curious to know the details of the cancellation and why he and his family, being at the end of the long waiting list, were to have the reservation. All the agent could tell him was that a cable had been received that morning from New York, offering passage for three. Neville wasn't the first to be contacted, but for reasons the woman couldn't explain, the other people she'd called were unable to sail in April.

Neville and his family sailed on April 20th and arrived in New York harbor on the first of May.

Just Imagine

A SUCCESSFUL FAMILY BUSINESS

*"Determined imagination is the beginning
of all successful operation."*
—By Imagination We Become

This is a striking story of an extremely successful businessman demonstrating the power of imagination. The businessman was Neville's older brother, Victor. The story began when Victor was eighteen and attending college out of the country. Their father, Joseph Goddard, was one of the partners in a merchandising business. His associates plotted against him, forcing him out of the business, and spreading false accusations against him, challenging his character and integrity. Because of it, he was deprived of his rightful share in the equity of the business.

Discredited and almost penniless, Joseph reluctantly called his son home. Victor returned, his heart bursting with one powerful resolution: He was determined to become extraordinarily successful in business.

The first thing he and his father did was use the little money they had to start their own company. They rented a small store on a side street not far from the large business Joseph had been part of.

Victor, with instinctive awareness that it would serve him, began to deliberately use his imagination. Every day he passed the building that his father's former business occupied. It was the biggest business of its kind in Barbados and one of the largest buildings in their city. On the outside was a huge sign with the name of the firm in large, bold letters. Day after day, as he passed by, a dream began to fill his mind. He thought of how wonderful it would be to own the distinguished building and have his family operating that great business.

One day, as he stood gazing at it, in his imagination he saw a different name on the big sign over the entrance. Now the letters spelled out their family name. He saw the name, letter by letter: J. Goddard & Sons.

Twice a day he gazed at the sign, coming and going to work at their little store-front business. Week after week, month after month, for two years, he saw the family name over the front of that building.

Victor truly believed that if he felt strongly enough that something was true, it would have to come true. He became convinced that one day they would own the building.

During this time, he told only one person what he was doing. He confided in their mother, who with loving concern tried to discourage him, to protect him from what she thought could be a big disappointment. Despite this, he persisted day after day.

After two years, the large company failed and the coveted building was up for sale. However, Victor was no closer to ownership than he had been two years before. He and his father had worked hard, and their customers had great confidence in them, but they didn't have the money required for such a valuable property. Nor did they have any source to borrow the necessary capital. On top of that, a number of wealthy business people were prepared to buy it.

On the day of the sale, to their complete surprise, a man they barely knew came into their shop and offered to buy the property for them. The man explained that he'd been watching them for some time. He believed in their ability, admired their integrity, and felt that supplying the capital for them to go into business on a large scale was an extremely sound investment for him.

All they would have to pay was six percent of the purchase price annually for a period of ten years, at which point they would pay out the loan.

They agreed.

That very day, the property was theirs. What a young man had persisted in seeing in his imagination was now a reality. The stranger's instincts had been correct, his investment rightly placed. At Victor's hand, the newly expanded business became extraordinarily successful, spreading across Barbados and many other islands as well.

Victor, seeing his family name over the entrance of a great building long before it was actually there, was using the very technique that produces results. By assuming the feeling that he already had what he desired—by making it a vivid reality in his imagination and tirelessly holding to his ideal regardless of appearance or circumstance—he inevitably caused his dream to replicate itself in his physical world.

SLEEP THERE NOW

"Sleep is the door into heaven. What you take in as a feeling, you bring out as a condition, action, or object in space. So, sleep in the feeling of the wishful filled."

—Feeling is the Secret

The following story illustrates how a student of Neville's prepared her dream home by imaginatively sleeping in it.

Margaret and her husband decided to put their current home on the market and find one big enough that they could invite Margaret's mother and her aunt to live with them. They also needed more room for their many pets. The new home would have to be very particular in size, location, and layout, as they wanted privacy for everyone concerned.

Several months and four or five real estate brokers later, her husband had given up on the idea of selling their house. Margaret knew from experience with imagining that their house wouldn't sell until they stopped "sleeping" in it. She still wanted to move, so for four nights in her imagination she went to sleep in the kind of home she wanted to own.

On the fifth day, her husband was at a friend's home and while there, met a stranger who "just happened" to be looking for a house that matched the location and description of theirs. After seeing it, he was eager to purchase. The couple moved within ten days and stayed with Margaret's mother while looking for their new home.

They gave their list of requirements to numerous agents, and each of them without exception told them they were crazy. They wanted an English style of home with two separate living rooms, separate apartments, a library, and it needed to have a large fenced yard for the dogs. Plus they weren't willing to look outside their preferred area OR pay more than they had budgeted. It was impossible, they were told.

Their list also included wood paneling throughout, a statement fireplace, a magnificent view, and privacy—they didn't want to be close to neighbors. Agents told them that no such house existed, but if it did, it would be five times what they were willing to pay.

Despite what she was being told, Margaret knew there was such a house—because she'd been sleeping in it in her imagination.

After two weeks, they'd gone through five real estate offices, and were meeting with a man in the sixth office, when one of his partners said, "Why don't you show them the place up on King's Road?"

A third partner laughed, "That property isn't even listed. And besides, the old lady would throw you off her land. She's got two acres up there and she won't split."

The couple asked to see it anyway as it was on the best street in their preferred area. As they drove up the street and turned into the private drive, they saw a large two-story house, surrounded by tall trees. Sitting alone and private on an expansive lot, it overlooked the city below. They felt a peculiar excitement as they walked up to the front door and were greeted by the owner who graciously asked them in.

Margaret couldn't breathe for the next moment or so because she'd walked into the most exquisite room she'd ever seen. The walls were solid redwood, and a magnificent fireplace rose over twenty feet to meet the cathedral ceiling which was graced with huge redwood beams. A picture window framed the sky, mountains, and city below them.

They were shown a spacious apartment on the lower floor with a connecting library, separate entrance, and separate patio. Two staircases led up to a long hall, opening into two separate bedrooms and baths. At the end of the hall was a second living room, opening out onto a second patio screened by trees. A fence enveloped the beautifully landscaped grounds.

That was just part of the property. The other half of the two-acre lot contained a large swimming pool and pool house completely separated from the main house.

As magical as it was, it seemed to be an impossible situation. As much as they loved the house, they didn't want two acres of highly taxable property with a swimming pool so far from the house.

Before leaving, Margaret walked through the magnificent living room again and went up the stairs. She looked down to see her husband standing by the fireplace, pipe in hand, with an expression of pure bliss on his face. She stood watching him for a moment.

Back at the real estate office, the agents were ready to close for the day, but her husband detained them saying, "Let's make her an offer anyway. Maybe she'll split the property. What have we got to lose?"

The agents present told them they were being ridiculous and recommended they forget about the place. Her husband who didn't usually get annoyed, slammed his hand on the desk and demanded they submit the offer. The agent reluctantly agreed.

That night in her imagination, Margaret stood on the staircase looking down at her husband by the fireplace. He looked up at her and said, "Well, honey, how do you like our new home?" to which she replied, "I love it!"

She stayed on the stairs, feeling the wooden railing and taking in the beauty of the room until she fell asleep.

The next day, during dinner, the phone rang and the agent, in an incredulous voice, informed them that they'd just purchased a house. The owner had split the property in half, giving them the house and the acre it stood on for the exact price they'd offered.

Just Imagine

MENTALLY CONSTRUCT IT

"Every image can be embodied. But unless you, yourself, enter the image and think from it, it is incapable of birth. Therefore, it is the height of folly to expect the wish to be realized by the mere passage of time."

—The Law and the Promise

The following is a story about a doctor and his wife who entertained a dream for years, but it wasn't until they entered into it, imaginatively, that they manifested it.

For fifteen years, Dr. Edmond had owned a lot that he'd built a two-story office building on. The building included his offices and a living area for him and his wife. There was ample space on the property for an apartment building—which they intended to build when their finances permitted. But after years of paying off the mortgage, they had no extra money for the additional building they still really wanted.

As they listened to Neville's teachings, they began to see that they could have what they wanted by controlling their imagination—and the idea of doing it without money was compelling. So they put it to the test, setting aside their current reality and concentrating on their powerful desire.

They mentally constructed the new building, just the way they wanted it. They even drew up physical plans so they could better form a mental picture of the finished structure. Keeping the completed, occupied building in their minds, they took many imaginative trips through their apartment house, renting units to imaginary tenants, examining in detail every room, and enjoying the feeling of pride as friends congratulated them on the unique planning.

One day, while talking about their building, his wife mentioned a contractor who'd constructed several apartment buildings in their neighborhood. She'd seen his name on signs in front of buildings under construction.

They quickly realized that if they were living in the end, they wouldn't be looking for a contractor, so they dismissed the thought. They'd been imagining daily for several weeks and both felt fused with their desire. They'd been successfully living in the end.

A few weeks later, a stranger entered the doctor's front office and introduced himself. He was the contractor his wife had mentioned weeks before.

He was somewhat apologetic as he said, "I don't know why I stopped here. I don't normally go to see people; people come to see me."

He went on to say that he often passed by the doctor's office and wondered why there wasn't an apartment building on the lot since there was more than enough room for one.

Dr. Edmond assured him he would like to have one there, but he didn't have money to put into the project.

The negative response didn't faze the contractor. He started to look for ways to make it happen—even though he hadn't been asked or encouraged by the doctor.

The doctor and his wife talked about the incident and then forgot it. So they were surprised when the contractor called, informing them that the project could go ahead and quoting an amount.

The couple thanked him politely but did absolutely nothing. They knew they'd been living imaginatively in the end of a completed building. They also knew that imagination would assemble that building perfectly without any intervention from them.

The contractor called again the next day to say he had a set of blueprints that should fit their needs perfectly with few alterations. This, he informed them, would save them the architect's fee.

The doctor kindly thanked him again and still did nothing.

Two days later, the contractor called again saying he had a finance company willing to cover the necessary loan. All the couple would have to pay up front was a few thousand dollars.

Again, they didn't act on it. They kept reminding themselves that the building was completed and rented, and they hadn't put one penny into its construction.

The contractor made one more visit to the doctor's office announcing he'd take care of the balance of the loan.

This time they did something!

They signed all the necessary papers, and construction began immediately.

All but one of the units were rented before completion. Dr. Edmond and his wife were thrilled by the seemingly miraculous events that had unfolded but didn't understand this one "flaw" in their imaginal picture. However, knowing what they'd already accomplished through the power of imagining, they immediately conceived another scene.

This time, instead of showing a party through the unit and hearing the words, "We'll take it!", they paid an imaginal visit to the people who had already moved into that suite. They allowed the new tenants to show them through the rooms and heard their pleased and satisfied comments.

Three days later that final space was rented.

Through a controlled, waking dream, the doctor and his wife positively altered their physical circumstances. They learned how to live in their dream as though it were a reality.

And although help seemed to have come from external means, the course of events was ultimately determined by their mental activity. The participants were drawn into their imaginal play because it was dramatically necessary for them to be a part of it. The imaginal structure demanded it. And the "players" entered right on cue.

Their desire of fifteen years was realized. (And it could have been realized any time during those fifteen years if they'd known the secret of imagining.) Their dream was objectified—and they didn't put one penny of their own money into it.

A BLIND GIRL'S JOURNEY

*"The movement of every visible object is
caused not by things outside the body but
by things within it which operate from
within outward. The journey is in yourself.
You travel along the highways of the inner
world."*

—Awakened Imagination

A blind girl named Joanna was living in San
Francisco and taking the bus to work. When
the busses were suddenly rerouted, it forced her to
make three transfers between her home and her office,
adding two hours to the length of her trip. She decided
to put Neville's teachings to the test. A car and driver
seemed the obvious solution to her problem, so she
said to herself, "I'll sit here and imagine that I'm being
driven to my office."

In her living room, Joanna began to imagine herself seated in a car. She felt the vibration of the engine,
imagined the typical car smells, enjoyed the move-

ment of the vehicle, and even touched the coat sleeve of the driver. She centered her imagination on being in the car and, although blind, viewed the city from her imaginary position.

The car stopped, and turning to her driver, she thanked him. He told her the pleasure was all his. Joanna stepped from the car and heard the dull thwack of the door as it closed behind her.

She took the same imaginary ride the following day, giving it all the joy and sensory vividness of reality, and a few hours later, a friend called to tell her about an article in the paper. It was a story of a man who was interested in helping the blind. Joanna phoned him and stated her problem. He was willing to help. He shared her story with his friend, and between the two of them, they were able to see that Joanna got to and from her office every day.

And on the first ride to the office, she turned to her good Samaritan and said, "Thank you very much, sir." He replied, "The pleasure is all mine."

AN ARTIST REVISES HER DAY

*"It is a most healthy and productive
exercise to daily relive the day as you wish
you had lived it, revising the scenes to
make them conform to your ideals."*
—Awakened Imagination

The following is a story of an artist who, through revision, was freed, not just from physical pain, but from animosity toward others.

Helena taught all day Thursday in the art school where she worked. Coming into her classroom after lunch, she saw that the janitor had left the chairs on top of the desks after cleaning the floor. As she lifted one down, it slipped from her grasp and landed sharply on the instep of her right foot.

Examining her thoughts, as she'd been taught, she realized she'd criticized the man for not doing his job properly. He'd recently lost his helper and probably had more work than he could handle.

The accident, she saw, was an unwanted gift that had bounced and hit her on the foot. Looking down, she saw that her foot seemed okay, so she forgot the whole thing.

At home that night, after working for about three hours on a painting, Helena decided to make herself some coffee. To her shock, she couldn't put weight on her right foot, and when she tried she was in severe pain. When she took off her slipper to look at it, the entire foot was a strange purplish pink, swollen out of shape, and red hot. She wondered if she might have cracked a bone when she dropped the chair on it earlier.

Rather than continue speculating, she decided to revise the situation as Neville had taught, even though she was in pain and trying hard not to be frightened.

Lying in bed, she arranged the bedding so it didn't touch her foot, then started to review her day. It was hard because her mind kept going to her sore foot.

She thought through her day and saw nothing to add or change regarding the chair incident. She did, however, recall meeting a friend on the way home from work. They'd known each other since they were kids, but for the past year, the man had made a point of not speaking to her. Helena always said hi to him anyway, and when he didn't answer, her thoughts would often turn negative.

Helena stopped right there and revised the scene. In her imagination, she said hi to him, and this time he answered, "Hi!" and smiled. Now she was filled with appreciation for the man. She ran the scene over a couple of times, went on to another incident, and finished up the day.

Next, her mind went to a concert her friend was performing in the following day. Helena had been looking forward to going, but now she could hardly walk.

She began to create a scene in her mind—feeling herself having a lovely time at the concert, and standing on her perfectly good imaginary foot for her friend's ovation.

She fell asleep happily imagining, and the next morning, as Helena was putting on her slipper, she suddenly remembered the discolored and swollen foot she had withdrawn from the same slipper the night before. Now when she looked at it, it was perfectly normal. The strangeness of the situation made her think that it had been just a really vivid dream.

While waiting for her coffee, she went over to her drafting table and saw all her brushes lying helter-skelter and unwashed, and she wondered briefly why she'd been so careless.

Just then, the full memory of the incident returned. She smiled. It hadn't been a dream after all, but a beautiful healing of both body and mind.

Helena knew that it required forgetfulness and forgiveness to bring about the new state she desired, so she'd thrown herself into imagination, escaping the grip that her senses had on her. Because of revision, what had been so painfully real was no longer so. And like a dream, it had quietly faded away.

CREATING HIS FUTURE

"All my reasonable plans and actions will never make up for my lack of continuous imagination."

—Awakened Imagination

At nineteen, Rick was a mildly successful dance teacher. He continued in that static state for almost five years. Then a woman talked him into attending one of Neville's lectures. He heard Neville say that imagining creates reality. He thought the idea was ridiculous and decided to disprove the thesis. He bought the book, *Out of This World*, and read it several times.

Still unconvinced, yet curious, Rick set a rather ambitious goal for himself. He was currently an instructor at an Arthur Murray Dance Studio, and his goal was to own a franchise and be his own boss.

At the time, franchises were extremely difficult to secure, not to mention he didn't have the necessary funds to launch such an operation. Nevertheless, Rick brought the dream to fruition night after night in his imagination. He went to sleep as the owner/operator of his own dance studio.

Three weeks later, a friend called him from Reno. His friend owned the Murray studio there and said it was too much for him to manage alone. He offered Rick a partnership. Rick flew to Reno on borrowed money, forgetting all about Neville, goals, and imagination.

He and his new partner worked hard and were very successful, but after a year Rick still wasn't satisfied. He wanted more. He began thinking of getting another studio. He tried to make it happen, but all his efforts failed.

One night, he couldn't sleep and decided to read. Looking through his collection of books, he noticed Neville's, *Out of This World*. It reminded him of his goal. He reread the book that night, and later, in his imagination, Rick heard an executive at the Arthur Murray Corporation praising the good job they'd done in Reno. The man then said he had a second location ready if they wanted to expand.

Rick re-enacted the imaginal scene nightly without fail. Several weeks later, it materialized. His partner accepted a new studio in Bakersfield, and Rick had the Reno studio alone. He was convinced now of the truth of Neville's teaching and vowed never to forget again.

He wanted to share the knowledge of imaginal power with his staff. He tried telling them all the wonderful things they could accomplish, but most of them were unconvinced.

One young teacher listened to his story but told Rick that his success probably would have come about anyway. He said the theory seemed like nonsense but added that if Rick could give him proof—something he could witness—then he would be convinced.

Rick took up the challenge and devised a truly fantastic test. The studio in Reno wasn't very significant in the overall system because of the city's size. At the time, there were over three hundred Arthur Murray Studios, most in cities with much larger populations. So Rick's test was to make his little studio the topic of conversation at the upcoming dance convention in three months time.

His teacher-friend was doubtful.

That night Rick mentally created his drama. He felt himself standing before a large audience. He was delivering a talk on creative imagining, and he could feel the nervous jitters. He also felt the audience's acceptance and heard the roar of applause as he left the stage. Then he saw Mr. Murray, himself, come forward and shake his hand.

Rick re-enacted the entire drama every night until it became so real it seemed like it had already happened! Three months later, his imaginal drama materialized down to the last detail.

His studio was the talk of the convention, and Rick did appear on stage just as he'd done in his imagination. But after it all, the young teacher remained unconvinced. He said it had happened too naturally. He was sure it would have happened anyway.

Rick wasn't fazed. The young teacher's challenge had given him further opportunity to prove what he believed. Amping up his goal, he was now determined to own the largest Arthur Murray Dance Studio in the world. His nightly routine was to hear himself accepting a studio franchise in a large city.

Within weeks, Mr. Murray called and offered him a studio in one of the biggest cities in America. He accepted and then set out to make his new studio the largest and greatest in the entire system. He knew it would happen. He just had to imagine!

Conclusion

"Causation does not lie in the external world of facts. The drama of life originates in the imagination."

—The Law and the Promise

The wisdom in this book applies to everyone, but your awareness of it is what makes it a powerful tool. The day you realize this great truth—that everything in your world is a manifestation of your mental activity, and that the conditions and circumstances of your life only reflect the state of consciousness you're fused with through imagination—will be the greatest day of your life.

Just as Neville discovered, you have an innate ability to feel what you desire to be. And as you feel it—giving it all the vividness and sensory fullness of reality—you become aware of being it. Then you walk as though you ARE it because you've taken your desire out of the imaginary world of possibilities and placed it where objective reality fills in the details.

You learn to ignore what is (if it's not serving you) because you understand that it's merely a temporary state. You accept the end, the fulfillment of your desire, as a reality rather than a far-off dream, and you become indifferent to the possibility of failure. You come to expect results. Then you start to manifest your own "Barbados" experiences.

Your imagination is not a state of being. It's so much more than that. It's who you are. Imaginary living is so far removed from ordinary existence that you'll begin to feel sovereign within the sphere of your own state of consciousness. The objects of your imagination will become your reality—a state so real that the subsequent physical manifestation will simply be a testament to the grandeur that came before it.

Others will play a role in the unfolding of your dreams, but you don't need anyone to give you your desire; it's yours now. Everything is here. Everything is now. It's all you, for you are God. And God is your wonderful human imagination.

"Our future is our own imaginal activity in its creative march."

—The Law and the Promise

About Neville

Neville Goddard (1905-1972) was part of the New Thought Movement in the United States. As a young man in New York City, he began studying under a teacher named Abdullah. Abdullah was born in Ethiopia and was of the Hebraic faith. He explained scripture in a way Neville had never heard before. He taught Neville about the power of imagination.

Neville went on to write numerous books, and taught and lectured across the country. He believed, as did Abdullah, that the Bible was a revelation of truth expressed in divine symbolism, a great psychological drama taking place in one's consciousness.

He taught that consciousness, being God, is the cause as well as the substance of the entire world; that our imagination is the gateway of reality; and that we can, through the law of assumption—with deliberate direction of attention and persistence of feeling—manifest a life of our choosing.

www.ingramcontent.com/pod-product-compliance
Lightning Source LLC
Chambersburg PA
CBHW021207020426
42331CB00003B/251